The Practice of Happiness
by John Kehoe

Zoetic Inc.
P.O. Box 48808
Suite 513 Bentall Centre
Vancouver, British Columbia
Canada   V7X 1A6

First edition June 1999

Second edition October 1999

www.learnmindpower.com

Canadian Cataloguing in Publication Data

Kehoe, John
The practice of happiness

ISBN 0-9697551-6-3

1.Happiness. 2.Self-realization. I. Title.

BJ1481.K44 1999   152.4'2   C99-900165-5

Printed and bound in Hong Kong
by Kings Time Industries Ltd.

THE
PRACTICE
OF
Happi

ness

contents

I dedicate this book to my father, who taught me the importance of happiness. A happy man himself, he was always supportive of me, no matter how strange or unusual my path seemed to him. Whenever he didn't understand my choices in life he would simply say, "John, you seem to be happy, and that's all that counts with me." With this unconditional support, I had the courage to follow my call.
Thanks Dad.

{
We shall not cease from exploration
And the end of all our exploring
Will be to arrive where we started
And know the place for the first time.
}

T.S. ELIOT

the Quest...

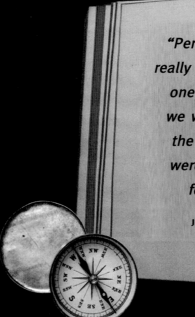

"Perhaps if one really knew when one was happy we would know the things that were necessary for our life."

JOANNA FIELD

Each of us wants

to be happy. Happiness is one of our most basic human desires, and yet so little is known or understood about happiness. What exactly is this feeling of happiness? What causes it? What makes it go away? Could it be permanent? These are important questions, yet few people seem to know the answers.

Is it achieving our goals which makes us happy? Is it health, wealth, personal fulfillment? One would think that having these things would make us happy, but it seems the answer is not so obvious or simple as that.

hap·pi·ness
(hap'ē nis), *n.*

1. *The quality of being happy.*

2. *The state of pleasurable content of mind.*

There are people who are in excellent health and yet desperately unhappy. There are multimillionaires who are miserable and people of very little means who are content. Some people are highly successful in their careers and yet they feel they have nothing. Others who have achieved much less are perfectly happy. Obviously there's more here than meets the eye.

So just what is it that brings happiness? Is there a secret to happiness, and if we knew this secret, would we then forever possess this elusive quality? Many years ago I set out on a journey to seek answers to these questions.

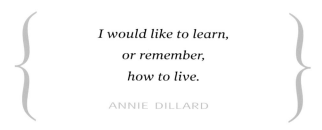

I would like to learn,
or remember,
how to live.

ANNIE DILLARD

Now, twenty years later, I've traveled to over sixty countries. I've spent time in Himalayan hermitages with Buddhist monks, in jungles with African healers, in sweat lodges with North American Indian shamans. Many wise men and women, in many distant places, have assisted me in unraveling the mystery of happiness. However, as you will discover in this book, the greatest truths are often revealed to us in the course of simple everyday experiences. Ironically, the secret of happiness was given to me by a man who lived not far from my own home. Its message can be summed up in one sentence. Indeed, in this text I will share with you the exact sentence that awakened within me the answer I'd been looking for.

Once you hear it you too will possess the key to your own happiness.

In my personal quest, I also discovered that there are certain practices that help us to obtain happiness. The wisdom of these practices was instilled in each of us at birth. As children we naturally knew and practiced them, but unfortunately, as we grew older and became adults, we lost touch with them. The good news is that since we still know them instinctively, once rediscovered, these practices are easier to learn and perform than you might suspect. The practices I'm speaking of are daily habits that you invite into your life, like you would an old friend or wise teacher. And you will find that each practice, when mastered, will indeed become a friend and teacher.

Each of us will naturally gravitate to some practices over others. Trust this process. No two paths in life are the same, and while all the practices lead to wisdom and happiness, some will be more relevant to you than others.

Before you continue, I want to give you an important insight that will point you in the right direction and assist you on your journey. Happiness exists within. You are the catalyst to your own happiness. But now I'm getting ahead of myself. Carry on, and read each chapter carefully. Take your time. This book is to be enjoyed and savored. You are now on the quest that each human being embarks upon from the moment of their birth. The search for meaning, purpose, and happiness.

WELCOME TO THE JOURNEY

follow
the call...

> *There is a forgotten promised land somewhere here, no, not a land, not promised, not even really forgotten, but something calling to you.*
>
> AMOS OZ

I am twenty-one,

living in Toronto, riding the streetcar to work while reading Henry Miller for the first time. I'm a claims examiner at Allstate Insurance. It isn't a particularly exciting job, but it's okay, and besides, you have to do something with your life.

Each day I take the Queen Street streetcar to work and get off at Bay Street. This particular morning I am totally immersed in Miller's book–his writing style, his life as an artist, his freedom, his courage to pursue what he believed in, even though he was sometimes hungry and always broke and no one would publish his work.

I have to catch myself, looking up a number of times to make sure I don't miss my stop, when the most delicious thought enters my mind. What if I don't get off? What if I just stay on the streetcar and don't go to work? It is an outrageous idea. And then I think how irresponsible this would be. People are counting on me. I have files to attend to. You can't be selfish, I tell myself; if you're going to quit do it properly and give notice. But the thought will not go away.

It is a beautiful spring day, unseasonably warm; the sun is shining and I feel alive with possibilities. Bay Street is now just two stops away and I don't know whether I'm going to get off or not. One stop away and still I don't know. Strangely, there is no inner dialogue. No arguing back and forth. It is like I'm watching a movie with myself in it; I'm totally unaware of what is going to happen.

Suddenly I'm at my stop. The scene is charged. I am at a crossroads, a point in destiny. The door opens. Am I getting out or not? I don't know. I'm in Fate's hands.

And here it's as if time slows. The door seems to remain open forever; there is plenty of time to get out. Then, finally, it closes and the streetcar lurches on. I sit in my seat, totally amazed at what has happened.

I ride the streetcar for another twenty minutes. I'm in unknown territory now. Seeing a park I get out, find a bench and continue to read Henry Miller. Sometime in the afternoon I call the company and quit on the spot.

About a month later I went back to pick up whatever pay was owed me. Over the next three years I wrote my first novel, which was never published. However, this led to a writing career, and now, four books later, I can safely say I'm a successful writer.

Recently I was telling this story to a friend of mine, a Jungian psychologist. "And what do you think would have happened if you'd got off the streetcar?" he asked. "I'd probably be manager by now," I responded instantly from somewhere deep inside myself, shuddering at the thought.

To discover your happiness you must first discover what pleases you, that place where your heart leaps for joy. This is your first clue. Follow your instincts–they are within you for a reason. They are the signposts to an exciting and fulfilling life. Choose paths that feel appropriate to you and follow them wherever they lead. There is a journey and adventure ahead, no matter what your age or circumstance. You are being called, and opportunities will always make themselves available to you when you follow this call.

And the call is made not just to the young.

I read a book many years ago (the title I forget) about a woman who left her husband when she was in her early sixties. It was a true story, chronicling how she made the decision, the horror of her children, all middle-aged, as they tried to talk her out of her foolishness, her uncertainty as she set out with only the clothes she could carry in one suitcase and a few thousand dollars. She left the house, the investments, all the valuables with

It takes courage to do what you want. Other people have a lot of plans for you.

JOSEPH
CAMPBELL

her husband. The book told the story of her adventures, both good and bad, ending four years later in a vineyard in Italy, with her happily married to a farmer and living a new and fulfilling life.

She did not heed her friends' advice that life was over, and so further destinies awaited her. She had the courage to leave a chronically complaining husband and a marriage that was barren, to trust the call within.

Each of us is called to be courageous and trust the voice within. You cannot fake it; you know clearly when you're following the call and when you're not. And, as the above story illustrates, we are called to be brave and courageous at every stage of our life. Every day, for that matter, gives us opportunities to be authentic and bold.

> *I know that I am august*
> *I do not trouble my spirit to vindicate itself*
> *Or be understood*
>
> WALT WHITMAN

When you rationalize, when you give in to fear, play it safe or let others decide for you, something is lost. There is a hole in you that nothing can fill. You know that you have refused the call. Others may not know; in fact they may compliment you on your decision, but you know. And each day that you try to deny it, you feel your integrity, your purpose, your lust for life leaking out through that gaping hole.

But when you follow the call every cell in your body is alive. There is an amplification of life and consciousness. Even if things are collapsing all around you, you feel invincible, like a warrior on a chariot, and everything within you is saying yes. You may not know what your next step is, but the adventure has begun, and what an adventure. "Fortune favours the bold," Rupert Murdoch said, and he is right. There is providence, a sequence of events that happens when you have the courage to heed the call. You will find that doors open, opportunities appear and helping hands are offered every step of the way. Does this surprise you? It should not, for you are now being guided by the star that burns bright within. And following this star will lead you to your happiness.

Not all destinies are ours to live and explore, but neither is there just one. We all have within us hundreds of possible destinies. Depending upon your unique circumstances, numerous opportunities will be made available to you when you act boldly. You are never stuck. Life is always giving you choices.

HAPPINESS

SZCZĘŚCIE

{POLISH}

You need not apologize for being you. To discover who you are and to become more and more you is your purpose in life. Do not trouble yourself about being misunderstood. It is bound to happen. This too is part of the path. Being one hundred percent authentic and true to your vision will undoubtedly offend some. It's the price you pay, but it's a small price for what you gain.

In fact, if you're pleasing everyone all the time, you're probably not being true to yourself. While you should not go out of your way to offend

Who do you think you are? A superstar?
Well, right you are. And we all shine on.
Like the sun and moon and stars.
We all shine on.

JOHN LENNON

or displease people, in some ways you can use this as a barometer. If absolutely no one is upset or displeased with your choices in life, I would consider that a bad sign.

Practice pursuing and following your uniqueness. This is your first call, and it is also your gift to the world. For following the call is never selfish. The voice within sees not just what is best for you, but also how you can best contribute to the greater whole. Paradoxically, we can offer greater contributions by being true to ourselves, by honoring the vision we have in our hearts, than we ever can by staying with something that violates our sense of individuality.

Who you are is far more unique than you would suspect. Your uniqueness goes far beyond your physical appearance. Just as no two faces are the same and no two fingerprints are identical, so too with your thoughts, your dreams, your aspirations, your beliefs; all these carry your individual imprint. Your experiences in life are unique. No one has lived a life like yours before. Nor will anyone have your particular opportunities. This fact is not to be ignored. It is the uniqueness of your life's journey that gives you the potential to contribute so much.

Candy Lightner discovered this when her life was turned upside down by the death of her twelve-year-old daughter. Her daughter was killed when a drunk driver broadsided the car Candy was driving. Candy's grief turned to rage, and then to action. She lobbied Congress to pass tougher laws against drunk driving. She founded MADD (Mothers Against Drunk Driving) and spoke all over America. Many changes were made because of her efforts. Destiny called to her; she heard the call and acted. Now the roads are safer for all of us.

All the solutions to the world's problems, all the social and environmental problems, the cures for cancer and AIDS, all lie within the consciousness of the human tribe. Each of us has been given a piece of the puzzle to bring forth, and we are all called to do so. If we fail to go within and bring out our unique contribution, then this contribution, whether large or small, will be lost forever.

Not all of us are called to be Martin Luther King, John Kennedy, Albert Einstein, Beethoven, or Nelson Mandela. But we are all called to be ourselves and to follow that path wherever it leads. Perhaps our call is that of the householder–to raise a family, to bring love, encouragement and vision to our children. In the Hindu tradition the role of householder is held in the highest esteem. And if you follow this path, like all worthy vocations, further adventures lie within.

There is a deeper, mysterious part of ourselves that transcends our day-to-day living. This other part of us seems to contain wisdom and understanding beyond what we can easily comprehend. If you are religious you might call it God. Or perhaps you might call it your Guardian Angel. A psychologist might call it the subconscious mind. Terms such as the inner self, intuition, sixth sense are also widely used. It doesn't matter what you call it as long as you realize there is a guiding part of yourself that is always available to you.

Quite often in times of great tragedy we will hear it more clearly. Or at destiny points in our life, like when I was riding that streetcar down Queen Street, it will call to us. Prayer, meditation, quiet times when we move beyond the busyness of day-to-day life in order to be refreshed from within, all these practices will help us hear our inner voice.

Even the simple awareness that this part of us exists makes us more receptive. When we live life with this awareness we are apt to trust our instinct and act upon what "feels" right. When something speaks within us, we listen, and then we ask ourselves if we have the courage to follow where it leads. But always the inner voice is there, calling us to fulfill our uniqueness, to become greater, happier and more full of life than we ever believed possible.

. life is a
journey
and it's
happening
now

"These are ancient

Aboriginal relics," the stranger says, handing me a wooden box containing what appear to be primitive, hand-held stone axe heads. He is dressed in shorts and a safari shirt, and tells me in a thick Aussie accent that he found them in the outback and feels that I should have them.

I have just finished my first Australian lecture on the powers of the mind and am standing to the side of a stage in Sydney, surrounded by numerous people who want to talk with me. Before I can question this man further, he mysteriously disappears back into the crowd, leaving me holding the artifacts.

During the next few months I often remove the stone objects from their box, hold them in my hands and imagine what history and secrets are contained within them. But, as I near my departure date, I find I have the distinct feeling that these relics should not leave Australia; they should be returned to their rightful owners. I contact an art dealer friend of mine, Tresham Stewart, who I know buys canvases from the Aboriginals. Several days later Tresham calls back to say an Aboriginal elder he knows will receive them. "Would you like to give them to him in person?" he asks.

On the flight to Darwin, looking out the window at the barren outback, I experience for the first time the true vastness of the Australian continent. And again the next morning, as the paved roads turn to dirt tracks, and eventually we're on no road at all, the sparseness of the landscape is both startling and strangely inviting. The outback seems to engulf us as we drive deeper into its heart.

The Jeep Tresham borrowed handles the rough terrain well, but as morning turns to afternoon the heat is becoming unbearable. After a long time of seeing no civilization whatsoever, we come to half-a-dozen shacks in varying degrees of disrepair. Children run out to meet us. They look dirty and their clothes are tattered, but their eyes blaze with life and curiosity. Immediately the Aussie flies, which I had heard so much about but which you don't experience in the city, attach themselves to me like leeches, crawling into my ears and nostrils. I swipe them away but within seconds they are back. The children laugh and mimic my frantic attempt to keep the flies off.

I am taken to one of the shacks. Inside are three men. The man in the

center seems to be the eldest. His face is painted with designs, the paint cracking and peeling off in tiny pieces. He is naked except for a loincloth tied around his waist. As I present him with the box I can't help thinking, "Who is this strange man and what am I doing here?"

The elder opens the box and takes each object into his hands, studying them carefully. Looking up at me, he stares intently into my eyes. It is as if he is looking deep into my soul, not at me but within me. Nothing is said for several minutes. I distinctly feel that he is reading my life. It is a strange sensation, but not at all unpleasant.

Finally he speaks to Tresham, who translates: "He would like to show you his gratitude. He wants us to spend the day and this evening he will perform a ceremony for you." I'm startled and don't know what to say. "It's a real honor mate. I've never known him to do this before," Tresham adds.

I agree and Tresham goes off to look at canvases while another Aboriginal wearing a T-shirt and jeans introduces himself. "My name is Sam. Are you hungry?" I'm ravenous, so he takes me to a makeshift kitchen and serves me what looks like stew. I am afraid to ask exactly what it is, but the flies obviously relish it. A swarm rises in the air as the ladle dips into the pot. I try to hide my reaction, but Sam, sensing my discomfort, says, "Don't worry. It adds to the taste." I'm not convinced. My voracious appetite has suddenly disappeared, but I don't want to offend my guests, so I force it down, all the while wondering if I'm about to die from food poisoning.

There was never any more inception than there is Now,
Nor any more youth or age than there is Now;
And will never be any more perfection than there is Now,
Nor any more heaven or hell than there is Now.

WALT WHITMAN

That evening we sit around a fire–the three elders, Sam, Tresham, my-self, and two women, one who must be at least eighty. The elder has fresh-ly painted designs on his face and body. Songs are sung, and although I do not understand the words, they seem to resonate deep within me. I had read that in days past the Aboriginals would follow "song lines," and dis-tances would be measured by the time it took to sing certain songs. With the songs having hundreds of verses, they were literally a kind of map. I wonder if these are remnants of those same songs.

"This ceremony is to awaken the love of the journey within you," Sam says. "My grandfather feels the white man does not respect the journey, only possessions. And you are a white man."

I am stung by his comments, feeling both wounded and indignant. But instinctively I know he is right.

Before I can respond, the elder stands and begins to dance amongst symbols that have been scratched in the dirt. He is surprisingly agile and seems almost in a trance as he methodically leaps from symbol to sym-bol. Sometimes he pauses on a symbol and chants. Other times he tra-verses many symbols while the others sing, and all the while the eerie sounds of the didgeridoo fill the night air. It is hypnotic and I am mes-merized, hardly aware of the hours passing. Abruptly the ceremony ends, and everyone disperses without further conversation or explanation.

Tresham pulls several wrapped blankets from the back of his Jeep. He and I spend the night on mats set out under the stars, with Tresham mut-tering, to himself as much as to me, "Never seen anything like it."

The next day Sam hitches a ride with us back to the city. On the way I ask him more about his grandfather's ceremony. By way of explanation, Sam tells me about the walkabout. "It happens with very little warning," he says, "someone in the tribe will 'feel' that it's time to go. Sometimes it's the night before, sometimes with just a couple of hours' notice."

Sam shares with us how these individuals then walk into the outback with just what they can carry. I learn that there's no particular purpose or meaning other than to walk about. There isn't even a destination. Sometimes the walkabout will be for a couple of weeks and sometimes a couple of months. No one knows how long it will last or where it will lead. "It's not about going somewhere; it's about the journey," Sam emphasizes. "Something happens when you abandon yourself to the journey without motive or destination. A transformation within takes place."

"Normally we don't talk of these things," Sam adds after a long silence. "But because you brought us gifts from our ancestors, my grandfather says you too should be given a gift. The ceremony was an initiation into the mystery of the journey."

I look at Sam but he is staring straight ahead. "In my people's tradition we believe each of us has our own journey. Each day is a step deeper into this journey. Each day is to be celebrated and honored," he says matter-of-factly, as if he's stating the obvious.

Sam looks at me to see my reaction. I begin to ask him another question but he stops me. "You cannot understand the journey with your mind. Only by living the journey will you know its truth," he says, and that's the last word he speaks until he jumps out at an intersection on the outskirts of Darwin, and says goodbye.

Looking back now almost twenty years to that day, I cannot say with certainty that the ceremony had a direct effect on me, but I suspect it did, for I spent the next twelve years as a virtual nomad, never living in one place longer than three months. And the love of the journey has never left me.

Life itself is the great journey. There is no destination. Our happiness depends upon understanding this. Each moment of every day is a part of this journey; each moment has the potential to fulfill us. Our family life, our work, our hobbies, our morning walk, time with friends, all these are excellent opportunities for experiencing moments of happiness. Within these simple daily activities is hidden the meaning of our life.

> { *Take no thought of tomorrow,*
> *tomorrow will look after itself.* }
>
> THE BIBLE

Jewish theologian Martin Buber tells a Hasidic tale about a teacher who lived an unusually abundant and happy life. After his death, one of his disciples was asked, "What was most important to your teacher?" The student answered, "Whatever he happened to be doing at the moment."

Can we possibly live our life day by day? This sounds too idealistic.

HAPPINESS

щастие

{RUSSIAN}

How can we take no thought of tomorrow? We have families, mortgages, commitments, plans. Are we to ignore these responsibilities? Not at all. They will always be there. We simply practice appreciating what is in our life today. We find joy today. We practice compassion today. We experience today fully. If we can do this, tomorrow naturally looks after itself.

> *There are no little things,*
> *'little things' are the hinges of the universe.*
>
> FANNY FERN

Our life is a continuous event, always with us, but we are not always with it. Where are we? In our minds. We're busy thinking about other things. Thinking about the past, which we can do nothing about. Making plans for a future that is not yet here. We're not noticing what is in front of us right now, not letting the fullness of the moment in. We must change this way of living.

We can never be happy in the past or in the future, we can only be happy now. Our call to enjoy life is now. Now is where we will always find ourselves. Now is where our life happens.

Many years ago, while traveling in Tibet, I witnessed a sand painting in progress. Daily, in a local market, the maroon-robed monks worked diligently, creating the intricate forms that made up the mandala. Different colored sands were used, and each detail was completed with the utmost attention. There were six or more monks working on it at any given time. Each day when I returned to the market, I looked forward to seeing what new designs had been created. It took more than a week to finally finish the painting. An elaborate ceremony followed, and then something totally unexpected happened. All at once the painting was destroyed. The hundreds of man-hours that it took to create this beautiful masterpiece were wiped away in a single moment. I was stunned.

This action defies our western sensibilities. Our western notion of labor is that we work in order to achieve a result. It is what we produce from our effort that is important. But to the Buddhist it is the process that matters, not the final achievement. It is the attentiveness to each moment. It is the journey of creating the mandala, and not the mandala itself that is important. There is a great lesson to be learned here, as we rush through our lives, striving to be successful.

Buddhist monks have been known to take this practice into prisons, doing sand paintings with the prisoners participating. While the inmates are often initially skeptical, something usually clicks and they embrace the practice enthusiastically. They find it relaxing, and strangely reassuring.

And it *is* incredibly reassuring. What could be more reassuring than to realize that our life has meaning, purpose and value not by what we achieve or possess, but simply because we are.

Zen Buddhism stresses the importance of living life moment by moment. Zen Buddhists have many meditations and practices that assist the student to experience this. One of these practices is to begin thinking of the Now not as a concept, but as a place you can go to. A different dimension, as it were. A dimension where one experiences the delicious sensations of Zen mind, child mind. Being fully aware. Letting go of our worries and expectations and relaxing in whatever moment of our life we happen to find ourselves in.

When the thinking mind is silenced in this way, even for a few moments, an extraordinary awareness occurs. Our reality is experienced in a direct way, without the filter of conceptual thinking. And what do we see and experience? Everything becomes grander and fuller. We discover that we need nothing more than what we have. We are amazed at how much beauty, joy, and wonder exist even in the most ordinary experiences.

It is a mistake to put off being happy. We've become so preoccupied with getting things done and trying to achieve our goals that we forget to be happy now. Then, when we achieve the goals that we thought were so important to us, we find that the happiness we had hoped to find is fleeting. Something more is needed. Buddha un-

Be on guard that you don't get sidetracked in the superfluous activity and not pay attention to the living of life.

JOSEPH
CAMPBELL

derstood this well. He taught that for every desire you fulfill, more desires will always come to take its place. This is the nature of life. You
will never be happy by simply achieving goals or gaining more possessions. Happiness comes by embracing the journey and appreciating our
life here and now.

Practice finding simple moments of joy and happiness each day. Notice
how many daily experiences are actually pleasurable. Think of happiness
as something to be experienced and enjoyed many times each day.

We have been looking to be happy and fulfilled and at peace with ourselves. We have been looking everywhere but where we are. We need
search no longer. Embracing our life, we discover that all is contained
within this very moment. This is an extraordinary journey we're on, and
it's happening to us Now.

Wherever you go there you are.

ZEN PROVERB

trusting
life

Faith isn't blind it's visionary.

"This is it," I say

to myself, my eyes feasting upon the pristine natural beauty of the marsh. I'm standing in the shade of towering red cedars; the sunlight gives a surreal, golden-emerald hue to their moss-covered branches, which in turn filter and disperse the light into a brilliant mosaic patchwork on the forest underbrush. A Great Blue Heron glides gracefully, silently in for a landing not twenty feet from where I am.

I've been looking for two months for somewhere to build my cabin. Nothing I've seen so far has felt right, but I knew the perfect place had to be out there somewhere, so I kept looking. Now at last I've found it. The site is totally isolated, yet close enough to a dead-end road that I can carry in all the necessary building materials. What's more I have permission to build here. Beavers have begun work on a dam close by. The symbolism of their building a new home where I plan to build a new life is not lost upon me.

A week later, the harsh reality of muling in countless loads of two-by-fours, sheets of plywood, roofing, literally everything, including a kitchen sink, is taking its toll. My original romantic image of building a cabin in the backwoods had somehow failed to include this part. It had also not included the mosquitoes. It is backbreaking work, but, persevering, I manage in ten weeks to have a basic A-frame cabin to the point where I can move in.

I lie in bed that first night listening to the beavers working diligently. The frequent slaps on the pond's surface let me know that their work is still in progress. Frogs–seemingly in the thousands–serenade the evening in ways I have never heard before. It comes in waves, starting with a few, then more and more until the entire pond is vibrating with sound. It has a mysterious rhythm to it, with crescendos and lulls and choruses. I am enchanted and overwhelmed, feeling as if I'm privy to one of nature's wondrous raptures.

I lie awake most of the night. I have now "arrived" at this new life, but I have no idea where it will take me. I've quit a well-paid job in Toronto and traveled nearly 3,000 miles to build this isolated cabin in the Pacific Northwest rainforest, where I now have no security, no plans, and no means of supporting myself.

When people ask, "Why are you doing this?" I have no answer. I usually just shrug or make up some reason, but really there is no reason other than that it feels right. I'm trusting that this feeling will lead me to something valuable, hoping that somewhere down the line it's all going to make sense. I'm operating on trust and instinct. I've never felt so vulnerable yet so sure in my whole life.

Little did I know that this period in the woods would last for three years and become the pivotal point of my life.

—·—

Why do some people make the leap of faith and others not? What is the decision-making process, the gut feeling, the overriding factor that allows one to defy the odds and go for the dream?

As children we were naturally brave and courageous. Our inquisitiveness led us to continually explore our world, to do new and different things. We never said, "I wonder if it's going to work out or not?" when trying something new. We just did it. We trusted life. But as we grew older we lost much of this ability.

Something happened and we began to distrust life. We came to distrust ourselves, our instincts, our dreams. This is unfortunate, because our fear and uncertainty about life often hold us in situations that are inappropriate. We hear the call but do not have the courage and self-assurance to follow it.

One of my favorite spiritual parables is that of the prodigal son. It tells the story of a young man who takes his inheritance and leaves his

father's house, soon falling into bad habits and ways. After a period of time he realizes his new life is not making him happy, but he is reluctant to return home, fearing condemnation for his actions. He finally finds the courage to return to the path that takes him back to his father, and when his father sees him coming from a distance, rather than chastising his son, the father rushes joyfully out to meet him, presents him with gifts, and orders that a feast and celebration be held in his son's honor.

Wouldn't it be ideal if life were really like that? Well it can be, but we must return to the ways of courage and innocence to experience it. Like the prodigal son, we too have fallen into bad habits and ways. We have allowed doubts, worry, indecision, fear, as well as a whole host of negative attitudes to take root within, and they prevent us from discovering the joy in our lives. Life will always be generous with us when we return to its natural ways.

The Muslims have a similar belief about trust. The Koran says that if you take one step towards Allah, Allah will take two steps towards you.

But always we are called to take that first step. And the first step is to move forward bravely in our life, like we used to do as children. To trust the process of life itself. To trust our instincts, our hearts, our passions, our dreams. To move ahead in life without needing to have all the answers, operating on instinct and faith.

Operate on the premise that things are going to work out, and they usually do.

The phone rang. It was a wrong number. Holly was about to hang up but something in the voice sounded attractive. She made a little joke, he did too and then there was silence, neither of them hanging up. "Want to talk?" he asked. "This is strange but why not," she thought, trusting her instinct, for she was not in the habit of talking to strangers on the phone.

Living is a form of not being sure, not knowing what next or how ... The artist never entirely knows. We guess. We may be wrong, but we take leap after leap in the dark.

AGNES
DE MILLE

Four hours later, as the sun was rising for Jeremy in the south of France, and it was late evening for Holly in Vancouver, both of them finally hung up, realizing something extraordinary had taken place.

A few days later Jeremy called back. They talked at length again, and a long-distance romance began.

Two months later Holly was at the airport to meet Jeremy for the first time. They had agreed to not exchange pictures, or describe their physical features, so neither of them knew what the other looked like. Holly waited anxiously in the arrival lounge wearing a purple dress and standing against a wall, just like they'd planned. Jeremy found her easily.

Holly brought Jeremy over to our place for dinner a few days later. The chemistry between them was obvious. "A couple of love birds," my wife said after they left. Sure enough, Jeremy proposed that week, and Holly accepted.

{ *There are only two ways to live your life. One is as though nothing is a miracle. The other is as though everything is a miracle.* }

ALBERT EINSTEIN

The wedding was in Vancouver, exactly six months after that first phone call. It was a warm, sunny day and the ceremony was held outdoors in a garden setting with friends and family of both present.

Holly and Jeremy are now living very happily in the south of France, surrounded by an olive grove and enjoying the pleasures of married life.

No one who knows Holly well is surprised that this would happen to her. Holly is a person who trusts life and expects the best. She quit a high-paying job to do legal administration work freelance. If money wasn't there one month she knew it would come the next. She always believed things would turn out well and they always did.

All our problems are made so much simpler when we learn to trust. There is a mysterious force and rhythm in life that comes to our assistance in the most unusual ways. And it comes more frequently and in greater abundance to those who have learned to trust the unknown.

We need to leave room in our life for the unexplained and mysterious. To trust that life is on our side, that good things can and will happen to us. Not all the time, but regularly and consistently enough for us to have faith in life.

I believe in miracles. I believe that there is a great mysterious force in life which defies logic and explanation, that sometimes the impossible is possible. Whenever I find myself in a truly difficult situation and there seems to be no possible solution, I ask myself, "Would it take a miracle to get out of this?" If I can answer yes, I immediately relax. "Oh that's all–just a miracle. And there I was getting all worried." Strangely this little practice is always reassuring to me. I can then ease off and let something else take over.

Acknowledging that our life is filled with mystery opens the door to the possibility of something totally unexpected happening to us, often when we most need it.

Like what happened to my brother-in-law Tim Allen.

"My wife Ellise and I were scuba diving in the Florida Keys on our honeymoon when my gold wedding ring slipped off my finger and disappeared into the muddy ocean bottom. I looked for it desperately but it was gone. "Back on shore, Ellise was distraught and crying. It certainly wasn't a very good omen. I knew right then that I had to find it.

"Early the next morning I went to the local dive shop and told them what had happened. I said I wanted to hire two divers and that the three of us would go down and look for the ring. They thought I was crazy. 'You've got a better chance of finding a needle in a haystack,' one of them said. 'Do you want my money or not?' I answered testily.

"We went out in the boat and anchored near where Ellise and I had been diving. I could see the look on their faces. They thought I was out of my mind, and in some ways so did I, but I had to try.

"It was agreed that if we didn't find it after an hour we'd surface. We all three jumped into the water.

"An hour later we had found nothing and our air was running low. They pointed to the surface, indicating it was time to go. I refused and kept looking. With my tank on empty, I turned over one last rock and felt in the mud. My hand felt something. I grabbed it and began surfacing. As I rose, I saw it was the wedding ring. Breaking the surface I let out the loudest cheer of my life. No one could believe it.

"Later that morning I pressed the ring into Ellise's hand. It was an emotional moment for both of us. Now in many ways this incident is a symbol of our marriage."

——

At certain points in our life we all must look deep within ourselves and ask the most fundamental of all questions: "Do I trust Life?" And you will hear the answer within. It will be either yes or no. Maybe the yes is loud and clear and it surprises you with its clarity and strength. Then again the yes might be the faintest of whispers, barely audible.

You struggle to even hear it, yet it is there. It has been forgotten and neglected for so long that you are relieved to hear that it is still alive within you. You rejoice upon hearing it. I have known grown men and women who have wept upon hearing it, because it gave them such courage and inspiration to carry on.

If, on the other hand, the answer is no, do not despair. A new challenge lies before you. The relationship has been strained. Someone or something has let you down. A healing is required. All relationships are built upon trust. So too with life. And you must take the first step.

HAPPINESS

SREĆA

{YUGOSLAVIAN}

Say Yes to Life.

Life is always calling to us to step forward and embrace the great teacher, the great parent, the source of all we experience. When we do this life supports us. We are never alone or without guidance, never without opportunities and choices. Trusting life lets us recover from tragedies. It empowers us to take chances. It gives us courage. When we trust life we can be more creative. Trusting life is the foundation of a happy and serene life.

Practice trusting the process of life itself. Notice how often problems work themselves out, how solutions always somehow appear when you need them most.

All you have to do is be still and take time to seek for what is within, and you will surely find it.

Life is supporting us in many ways; we've simply not been noticing. Often we fight the process by worrying and trying too hard. In doing this we're actually swimming against the tide. No wonder life can sometimes seem so hard. It's time to trust, let go and just flow. No matter what crisis or hardship you find yourself in, life will support you when you surrender completely to its mystery.

EILEEN
CADDY

{ *Just trust yourself, then you will know how to live.* }

GOETHE

good luck bad luck

{ *There are years that ask questions and there are years that answer.* }

ZORA NEALE
HURSTON

The front of my

car suddenly swerves to one side, wobbling violently. Gripping the steering wheel tightly, I bring the car to a stop and climb out. Sure enough, a flat tire. I thought I'd allowed enough time to make the ferry, but now it's going to be tight.

Working quickly I'm back on the road in fifteen minutes. I look anxiously at my watch. Maybe if I'm lucky I'll make it. Maybe the ferry will be running late. But rounding the last bend I see the ferry pulling out. "Bad luck," I say to myself, wondering what I am going to do until the next ferry arrives. It is Saturday morning and I am at Ganges Harbour, on Saltspring Island.

I wander down to the wharf, where a number of fishing and sailboats are tied up. I love boats and am always willing to spend time looking at them. A fishing boat tied up next to the dock is selling fresh Coho and doing a brisk business. Several pleasure craft are fueling and stocking up on supplies. A noisy group of seagulls are squawking and fighting over a piece of bread someone has thrown them.

At the very end of the wharf a classic wooden gaff-rigged cutter is bobbing in the wake of passing boats. I can see that it's in impeccable condition. The deck and cabin are cedar and there are wooden dowels holding the planking in place. A small FOR SALE sign in one of the portals catches my eye. It's a dream of mine to own a sailboat.

I step down to the platform where she is moored to have a closer look. Every detail of the boat is done with incredible craftsmanship. Someone has obviously spent a lot of time building this, I'm thinking, when suddenly the hatch opens and out pops a head. "Beautiful day, isn't it?" he says.

"Certainly is, and your boat's a beauty too," I reply, stepping back and admiring the rounded curve of the stern where the name *Akimbo* has been carved. "I'm Eddie," he says, "I built it. I was just about to go out for a sail. Want to join me?"

I don't need to be asked twice. Eddie unties the bow and stern lines and pushes us off. There is a slight westerly and the way the boat is positioned, we simply drift away from the dock. Eddie grips the halyard with his large hands and quickly the mainsail is up. He is strong and muscular, with a bushy beard. The mainsail sets and *Akimbo* heels over obediently.

The mast looks freshly varnished. It is gleaming golden yellow in the sunlight. Eddie sees me looking at it. "It took me two weeks to find the right tree for the mast," he says. "Nobody takes the time to build wooden boats much anymore. They're almost all fiberglass. No character," he adds wistfully, and then, just as quickly, his eyes twinkling, "A wooden boat has a soul."

We sail out Polaris Pass into Georgia Strait where the Coast Mountains, still snow capped from the winter, come into view. There is something about Eddie I can't quite figure. Although I've known him now for only the briefest time I'm sure he's the most peaceful, relaxed person I've ever met. He seems totally at ease with me, a complete stranger, in his boat. But there's more. He seems so in tune with what he's doing, and he seems to answer my questions even before I ask them. "I hate to sell her," he says, "but you seem like someone who would take good care of her." I haven't said anything about wanting to buy a boat. But he's right. I would love to own this boat.

Before I can say anything, Eddie exclaims, "The whales are here!" "Where?" I ask, standing immediately and looking in every direction. "I don't know," he says enigmatically, "but they're here somewhere. I can feel them."

I continue to look for a few moments, but see nothing. I sit back, neither of us saying anything, with only the rhythmic sounds of *Akimbo* cutting through the waves breaking the silence. Suddenly I hear a blowhole erupt behind us. I know from the sound that it's very close. I turn and a gigantic hump surges through the water within an oar's length of the stern. There is no head or fluke, just this massive mound of flesh slipping smooth and wet through the water, causing hardly a ripple. I can see the barnacles and scars on its blue-gray skin. There's a second one and then a third. It's a pod of three grays migrating north to the cool Alaskan waters for the summer. We look on in awe. Eddie moves the tiller and we try to follow them but they leave us behind within minutes.

"Our lucky day," says Eddie, beaming.

As it turned out, my chance encounter with Eddie was indeed incredibly fortunate. Not only was I soon to become the proud owner of the *Akimbo*, but he later taught me one of the most important lessons you can ever know about happiness. Meeting Eddie was one of the best things that ever happened to me.

And I met him only because I missed the ferry.

It's often hard to see our life in perspective while it's happening. So much is going on at any given time. It's often helpful to step back and

It is not until the later stages of our life that we look back and see that everything had a purpose and meaning.

JOSEPH CAMPBELL

allow the process to unfold in its own mysterious way, without immedi- ately categorizing each event in our life as either good or bad according to how pleasant or convenient it happens to be for us at that moment. Life is much more complex and multi-layered than that.

All incidents in our life have their purpose. Both fortune and misfor- tune serve us in their own way. We often do not understand at the time why certain events are happening to us, but everything plays a part in the formation of our character and fate. One can find wisdom and lessons in the most unusual places, and destiny is always at work, even in the most casual of encounters.

A hermit lived on the edge of a forest close to a small village. The villagers all thought he was a fool, for he spoke in paradoxes. His name was Jed. One day Jed took in a stranger who was sick and nursed him back to health. In grati- tude the stranger gave him a horse. When the villagers heard what had hap- pened they congratulated Jed.

FELICE

{ITALIAN}

> *"Jed, what good luck! What great fortune!"*
> *"Who knows if it's good luck?" Jed responded. "Maybe it's bad luck."*
> *"Bad luck?" they laughed. "How can it possibly be that? You had no horse; now you have one. This is good luck! What a fool," they thought, "he cannot even recognize good luck when it happens to him."*

Jed took his meager savings and bought a saddle. Then one day, the horse escaped and ran away.

{ *Everything that happens to you is your teacher. The secret is to learn to sit at the feet of your life and be taught.* }

POLLY BERENDS

"Oh, what bad luck," the villagers said when learning what had happened. "You now have a saddle and no horse."

"Who knows if it's bad luck? Maybe it is good luck," Jed responded cheerfully.

"Good luck?" they laughed. "There's no way this is good luck. This is a tragedy for you."

"Who knows?" said Jed.

Several days later the horse mysteriously returned and brought with him a couple of wild horses. Jed quickly led them into a corral, and word soon spread that he now had three horses. The villagers rushed to see for themselves.

"What good luck!" they said to Jed. "You now have three horses. You can sell two and keep one for yourself."

"Who knows if it's good luck," Jed said. "Maybe it's bad luck that this has happened."

"Bad luck?" they laughed, unable to hide their pity for such a simple-minded fool.

One day while attempting to ride one of the wild horses Jed was thrown and broke his leg.

"What bad luck," the villagers said when they learned of the mishap.

"Who knows," said Jed. "Maybe it's good luck that I broke my leg."

A week later an invading army stormed through the village and forcibly conscripted all the men who were in good health, but they did not take Jed because he had a broken leg.

It is an old parable and the story goes on and on. The message is clear: Who knows what is good or bad luck? The tragedy, setback, or misfortune you may now be experiencing might very well be the best thing that ever happened to you. Who knows?

We underestimate the value of crisis and misfortune. We want life to always be comfortable. But sometimes it is the carrot and sometimes the stick that gets us to move and change. Comfort is the enemy of change. We never make changes when everything is going well. Why would we? But when a crisis bangs down the door of our carefully planned reality, changes happen quickly.

Gracefully accepting whatever new circumstances are happening to us, no matter what they are, frees us to understand them. Instead of cursing and fighting an unpleasant situation, we allow it to have its place in our life. And when we let go of the struggle, both it and we undergo a change.

The Quaker Emmet Fox said, "Bless a thing and it will bless you. If you bless a situation, it has no power to hurt you, and even if it is troublesome for a time, it will gradually fade out, if you sincerely bless it."

Writer Sarah Ban Breathnach said, "There are only three ways to change the trajectory of our lives: crisis, chance and choice." She should know. During the mid 1980s she was a freelance writer and radio broadcaster and seemed to have it all, a career she loved, a family, her health; life was good. One day while taking her two-year-old daughter Katie to lunch at her favorite fast-food restaurant the roof caved in, literally. A large ceiling panel fell and struck her on the head. While relieved it did not hit her daughter; Sarah nevertheless sustained serious injuries.

A severe concussion left her bedridden, confused and disoriented for months, and partially disabled for a year and a half.

"They were dark months, both emotionally and physically. I lost track of time, my sense of rhythm, my identity, my feeling of safety. I felt imprisoned in my own body, sentenced to solitary confinement for an unspecified duration. I wasn't dead, but I wasn't alive."

During her long rehabilitation she began telling herself stories as therapy. "Although I had been a journalist for ten years, I had never thought of myself as a storyteller." This led to a new creative outlet and would later birth a new career. She published her first book, *Simple Abundance*, which stormed up the best-seller lists, and now she is a full-time writer, something that might never have happened to her were it not for the accident. Life works like that.

It is only natural to crave some stability in this fast-paced world of ours, but change is the truth and law of our being. Life needs change and movement, just as a plant needs sun and rain. Every aspect of our life–our health, our marriage, our work, our relationships, our beliefs–is constantly changing and becoming something else. If you trust life you must also trust change.

The only constant in our life
is constant change.

Whenever someone says to me they are going through a midlife crisis I always respond, "How wonderful!" and I mean it. How wonderful that at the "midpoint" of your life your psyche shakes you up and demands that you look at your life, your values, your goals. It makes you re-examine everything. This is an important process, especially at the halfway point of your life, where you still have so many opportunities ahead of you. We should be ever grateful that life forces these things upon us. Midlife crises are never enjoyable–they are terrifying and confusing (assuming that you're having a half-decent one); you go through anguish, despair, self-doubt–but they are always valuable. Always. When you come out the other side you have a clearer sense of what is important and what is not. Often your priorities change. What was once important becomes unimportant. What was inconsequential becomes urgent. What was ignored is now given the utmost attention. It's like a rebirth, a second chance. What a valuable thing to happen at this stage of your life.

Life has a way of always working itself out. Even the most horrific situations pass and become something else. Often in hindsight, after we have gone through a bad period, we are amazed at what strength and insight we have gained. And yet while we were going through those difficulties we saw none of this.

In *The Teachings of Don Juan* by Carlos Castenada, Don Juan, a Mexican sorcerer, says, "The basic difference between an ordinary man and a warrior is that a warrior takes everything as a challenge, while an ordinary man takes everything as either a blessing or a curse." There is great truth in this. We need to move beyond judging everything as either good or bad, and accept the changes in our life, no matter what they are, as friends, teachers and opportunities.

Practice maintaining this perspective of openness and acceptance in all situations, and peace and serenity will come to you. There is great wisdom to be found when one approaches life with humility, knowing there is much we do not and will not ever understand. Accepting this gives us strength. We can be more relaxed and at peace with the turmoil and uncertainty in our daily life, trusting that everything will work itself out. The true alchemy in life occurs when we accept that every situation is there to serve us in some way, when we free ourselves to participate fully in our adventure.

{
Every period has something new to teach us.
The harvest of youth is achievement; the
harvest of middle age is perspective;
the harvest of age is wisdom.
}

JOAN CHITTISTER

Gratitude

{ *These are the good old days.* }

CARLY SIMON

It's the coldest

winter anyone can remember and the wood stove that heats my cabin has burned out again, leaving me freezing. In the kitchen I discover that the loaf of bread I mistakenly left out last night has had the corner chewed off.

No matter what I do to get rid of the rodents, it seems they always return. I'm reluctantly coming to the conclusion that I'll just have to share my food with them. Everything seems to be going wrong. My money is running low and I'm not sure where I'm going to get more. I'm in a miserable mood this morning. I can't think of one thing that's right in my life.

Maybe a walk will help. It's a twenty-minute hike from the cabin to the dead-end road where the mail is dropped off. I haven't checked in over a week. I'm hoping there will be some mail.

I open the box and pull out a single envelope. It's a letter from my friend Rin Chin. I wonder what he's up to. Anxious to hear his news, I begin reading right there at the mail box, but immediately I realize it's not good. He has had a horrible car accident and has lost his left leg. It has been amputated above the knee. I'm in a state of shock as I walk back to the cabin.

This is a man who has traveled the world, always taking the more adventurous, physically demanding route. Hiking, backpacking, mountaineering have been a way of life for Rin Chin. For him this must be a terrible blow. It would be devastating for anyone to suffer this sort of setback; for Rin Chin I know it is truly a catastrophe.

Gratitude makes sense of our past, brings peace for today, and creates a vision for tomorrow.

MELODY
BEATTIE

Stopping at the woodshed I'm thinking about how difficult my next letter to Rin Chin will be. What do you say? Picking up several pieces of wood to carry back into the cabin, it suddenly occurs to me just how fortunate I am. I have not one, two, but hundreds of pieces of wood to keep me warm, a cabin in a beautiful setting, my health and... two legs. I have so much.

That evening, lighting my kerosene lamp, instead of bemoaning the fact that there is no electricity, which I often do, I find myself suddenly grateful that I have a kerosene lamp. I could be in darkness. This morning I was miserable; now, although I'm still dismayed at my friend's misfortune, I'm feeling grateful and happy to be alive. Yet nothing in my circumstances has actually changed, only my perspective.

Then it strikes me. Maybe it's *all* perspective. Maybe it's not our circumstances at all, but how we *think* about our circumstances that makes the difference. And if this is the case, then how we view ourselves and our life is incredibly important.

Pursuing this train of thought, I decide that, instead of focusing on what's wrong, I'll make a list of all the things that are "right" in my life. Fifteen minutes later I'm astonished at how many things I have to be grateful for. Even Rin Chin has things to be thankful for, I realize. There and then I make a promise to myself to find something to give thanks for each day, no matter how desperate my situation may seem.

Twenty-five years later I've rarely missed a day.

A new life is but a new mind.

JAMES ALLAN

Every life has something to be grateful for. If we cannot find things to be thankful for then the reason lies within us. How have we allowed ourselves to become so hardened or desperate? Our inability to find joy or happiness in our life doesn't suggest in the slightest that joy and happiness are not there. Rather it suggests we are not looking carefully enough. It suggests that either we're not taking the time, or that our perspective is too narrow and limited.

Discovering joy in our lives comes from appreciating very simple experiences. We are not talking here about how good it feels to earn a million dollars, have your book make the best-seller list, buy a new car, or finish some major project that you've been working on for several months. These all bring feelings of happiness, but beyond these larger accomplishments, everyday life contains plenty of things to be thankful for. There is a fundamental goodness in just being alive which does not depend on attaining goals or fulfilling desires.

There is an old Shaker hymn that begins, "'Tis a gift to be simple, 'Tis a gift to be free." And simplicity does bring freedom. But simplicity does not necessarily mean doing without or cutting back. True simplicity is internal not external. It is an awareness that allows the ordinary to become extraordinary. Simplicity means needing less to be content. It means letting simple everyday experiences please us and bring us joy.

We have many of these moments each day. These events may take a fraction of a second, but they are very real experiences of joy and wonder. They happen all the time, but usually we ignore them, considering them mundane or purely coincidental. It could be a song you hear on the radio, a piece of writing that inspires you, the sight of two elderly people holding hands, a bird hopping across your backyard, the sound of your children playing in the next room, a good joke, a shared moment of intimacy with a friend; all these experiences will bring us joy if we allow them to. These experiences are treasured gifts to us, and we should not be so busy that we miss them. This takes diligence, because it is so easy to miss them.

Too often instead of appreciating the numerous blessings of our life, we get into the habit of focusing only on our problems. We complain that we're not receiving what we think we should. The simple day-to-day pleasures, which are always there for us, are either taken for granted or ignored. We find ourselves feeling neglected, deprived, overwhelmed, and stressed. When this happens we need to pull back and put it all into a larger perspective.

We need to remind ourselves that many pleasurable moments exist each day in our life. Understanding this, we make a decision to start noticing them. We take a few seconds here, a moment there, to stop and appreciate the small joys and beauty in our lives. And far from this being a chore, we find ourselves refreshed and nourished by this simple practice.

HAPPINESS

MASAYA

{FILIPINO}

Arise and drink your bliss!
Fore everything that lives is holy.

WILLIAM BLAKE

A friend of mine recently shared a remarkable story with me. The newspaper where he worked wanted a pictorial to illustrate the poverty and misery of the seedier parts of the city. Rather than sending out a professional photographer, my friend had the brilliant idea of handing out disposable cameras to the residents themselves, and asking them to take the pictures. He picked out a dozen drug addicts, alcoholics, petty thugs and inhabitants of flophouses, and instructed them to "shoot whatever you want. Share your life with us."

{ *I like living. I have sometimes been wildly, despairingly, acutely miserable, racked with sorrow, but through it all I still know quite certainly that just to be alive is a grand thing.* }

AGATHA CHRISTIE

He was not at all prepared for what came back. "When we developed the film," he said, "I was amazed at the hope and joy and beauty of the pictures. One was of a birthday party with a toothless old man blowing out the candles. Another was of a passionate kiss between lovers. Another was of friends preparing a meal. These pictures represented life lived with dignity and joy. It was not what I was expecting."

If even the most destitute can find joy and beauty in their lives, what then is our excuse? Are we any less fortunate?

No matter what our situation, there are moments of beauty and joy when we can live our life with inner dignity. This truly struck home for me when I traveled through India. I saw much poverty, and yet, despite this, many times dignity, honor, and beauty shone through. One particular incident occurred in Jaipur, a sprawling city in the north. It was evening and I watched as a man claimed a piece of the sidewalk as his home for the night. He laid out a rug and set up a small altar and arranged his few belongings. He did it with such dignity, his face serene. It was clear that in his mind he was suffering no misfortune. In fact he seemed quite pleased with himself. To my western eyes he was homeless and destitute, but in his mind he was at peace with himself and the situation. I learned a lot in that moment.

The GUEST HOUSE
by Rumi

This being human is a guest house.
Every morning a new arrival.
A joy, a depression, a meanness,
Some momentary awareness comes as an unexpected visitor.

Welcome and entertain them all!
Even if they're a crowd of sorrows, who violently sweep your house
Empty of its furniture,
Still treat each guest honorably.
He may be clearing you out
For some new delight.

The dark thought, the shame, the malice,
Meet them at the door laughing
And invite them in.

Be grateful for whoever comes,
Because each has been sent
As a guide from the beyond.

How many enjoyable experiences do we have in a life? Too many to even count. How many great moments? Sunsets, walks in nature, drives in the country, romances, friendships, good meals, celebrations, stimulating conversations, great songs. Adventures, goals achieved both small and large. Hundreds of thousands of enjoyable experiences. And how many times did we give gratitude and thanks for these experiences? Did we appreciate them while they were happening, or is it only in hindsight that we realize they were good times.

The trick is to appreciate what is happening to us in life while it's happening. Maybe we don't have everything we want? Few people do. Maybe things could be better? Things can always be better. Maybe we've got problems? There are always problems. But that doesn't stop us being grateful for what we do have.

There is a hidden hierarchy in life which dictates that gratitude for what we already have always precedes the attainment of that which we still desire. Gratitude always comes first, and gratitude can start right now, today, in our not-so-perfect life.

The power of gratitude cannot truly be appreciated until you have practiced it regularly. The vibration of gratitude transforms lives. All change in our life begins from within, and when we make a conscious decision to be grateful for what we already have, even if what we have is very little, we set in motion vibrations that attract more to us.

This is the magic of gratitude. It attracts more of whatever we give thanks for. If we praise and give thanks for our health, greater health will come to us. If we take the time to praise and give thanks for the ordinary moments of joy and happiness, even more of these moments will appear. Gratitude not only multiplies that which is praised, it increases the blessings in other areas of our lives as well. This is the truth and wonder that each person awakens to when they regularly practice gratitude. And for this realization, we should give great thanks.

*The eyes
of my eyes
are opened.*

E.E.CUMMINGS

the giveaway...

> There is no duty we so much
> underrate as the duty of being happy.
> By being happy we sow anonymous
> benefits upon the world.
>
> ROBERT LOUIS STEVENSON

It's early afternoon

and already several hundred people have arrived. Children are running everywhere, playing games and getting into mischief. Women are brushing marinade onto fresh salmon and preparing other delicacies for a feast.

Men are carrying boxes, cutting firewood, sharing stories and just catching up on news. It is a hive of activity in preparation for the potlatch.

The potlatch is the North American Indian "giveaway." I'm here with my friend Sun Bear, a Chippewa medicine man. Sun Bear tells me that in the old days, when any one family or individual accumulated substantially more material wealth than the other residents of a village, a potlatch was given.

The prosperous individual then gave away much of his material possessions, dispersing them to his various neighbors so that balance returned to the village. "Nowadays," he says, "it's more a way of sharing some good fortune, or just saying thank you to your community."

We are all invited to sit in a circle around a huge fire. Four drummers keep a steady beat on a large drum, and dancers in full-feathered regalia enter the circle to the beat of their drum. The host family follows the dancers, each member carrying a gift. The gift is then given away to someone in the circle. After each round of the circle, a new gift is gath-

ered up and again given away. There is excitement and anticipation as everyone wonders who is going to receive what gift. An old woman is given a beautiful hand-woven shawl and she smiles with obvious delight, bringing it to her wrinkled face to feel its soft luxury. Blankets, homemade preserves, smoked salmon, baskets, transistor radios, games; some items are homemade, others store-bought, but the gifts just keep coming. Hundreds of them. Sometimes it seems predetermined who is going to receive what; other times it is totally spontaneous. I am surprised when I am given a necklace, then, a half-hour later, a small blanket. We set our gifts in front of us. It goes on for hours. No one is left out. Everyone receives something, some people a lot.

Later that evening, after we'd all enjoyed a magnificent feast, I express my gratitude to Sun Bear for bringing me to the potlatch, telling him what a moving experience it has been for me.

"There is actually a greater giveaway than the potlatch that each of us is called to perform," he says. "This giveaway happens within but it is even more important. We are to give away our fear, our worry, our hates and grudges. Give away all that weakens us and pollutes the stream of consciousness." Intrigued, I ask him to explain further.

"Within each of us a great stream of consciousness flows. This stream, if it is pure, will nourish the human tribe. If it is polluted, it will make us sick. In these times that we are living in today, we are polluting the stream by how we think. We need to change our ways, our values. We must purify the stream to heal both ourselves and Grandmother Earth, and this giveaway can only be done one person at a time."

In that moment, Sun Bear gave me something far more valuable than any possible material gift. He pointed the way to a new understanding of consciousness.

> *People will give away almost anything, even their most valuable possessions, but they resist giving away their own problems.*
>
> GURDJIEFF

Sun Bear was a healer, and a very good one too. Many people came to him for healing. Sometimes he would sit by the person and sing healing songs to their bodily organs, talking to their cells and tissues as if they could hear him. At other times he would smudge them and send them off to the sweat lodge. Or perhaps he would give them herbs. But regardless of what method he used, he always first followed a certain ritual.

"First what I want you to do," he would say, "is to go out to the woods. Dig a hole and sit in front of it. Release from your mind all the hates, grudges, guilt and resentment that you have within you. Put these things in the hole, cover it up and come back without that stuff in you." And he would send people off to do just that.

He was encouraging the person to release all the toxic substances that were choking them from within. Sun Bear felt inner healing always preceded outer healing, and the power of this symbolic act was often enough to help the person give away that which was harming them. Then and only then could a true healing take place.

We too are obliged to purify ourselves and get rid of our own particular inner toxins. For inner harmony and happiness are not just for ourselves; they are gifts that we give to the world. And here a great truth is revealed.

Each of us adds to or takes away from the whole of consciousness by the way in which we think. Our strength adds strength. Our weakness weakens the whole. Just as a pebble dropped into a pond causes ripples to spread throughout the entire pool, so too does our thinking cause ripples throughout the whole of human consciousness.

geluk

The next great evolutionary advance for the human species will be a leap in consciousness. Such a major shift is not only possible, but is happening now, even as you read this book. Usually evolutionary changes happen over thousands of years, involving minute changes essentially imperceptible to the human eye, yet this incredible shift in consciousness is so profound that we can actually witness and feel its effect. The spiritual hunger, the search for a more balanced and meaningful lifestyle is not just happening to you, but millions of others as well. We are all being lifted and changed by an invisible tide.

{DUTCH}

It is no coincidence that our consciousness is shifting as the stakes are raised in our problem-filled world. This is nature at work at its finest. We are lucky, those of us alive in this time of accelerated human evolution. To be able to consciously participate in the Great Awakening is a unique honor and privilege, but we all must step up and play our part.

If we think of ourselves as socially responsible but ignore our own inner kingdom, we are fooling ourselves. Disharmony within is not a private act.

We need to ask ourselves, "Where have I been polluting? What needs to be given away?" We need to take responsibility for our attitudes and feelings. To give away that which no longer serves us. To give away our fear, our unhappiness, our depression, our hate, and our disrespect for ourselves and others. By doing this we are not only helping ourselves, but also actively participating in the evolution of consciousness.

Recently I was speaking at a university and sharing these same ideas. I said that the root problem of all environmental pollution–the killing of the whales, drift net fishing, industrial waste–lay not with the decisions of big companies and governments, but with our own inner disharmony. "The negative thoughts we entertain in our consciousness are what is creating these problems," I said.

One woman in the audience took immediate offence at this. She disagreed with me vehemently. "I'm not killing the whales!" she shouted, standing up. She began to list the environmental groups she belonged to, and all the good work she was doing. I tried to respond but she wouldn't let me. She quickly worked herself into a rage, and for the next few minutes the worst type of venom spewed from her mouth as she denounced both me and my ideas. Obviously I had touched a raw nerve with her. As her anger turned to rage you could feel the atmosphere of the whole room become charged with toxic energy. When she was finished she stormed out of the room, calling me several obscenities as she left.

The room became eerily silent. Nobody said a word. Everyone was wide-eyed, aware and clear. We looked at one another knowingly. What I had been talking about in theory was no longer just a concept. We had all just witnessed it in action and felt its effect. I couldn't have asked for a better demonstration. Everyone "got it" instantly. It was a great revealing moment for everyone present.

Two monks were on a journey when they came to a river where a beautiful woman was waiting. "Will one of you kind monks carry me over to the other side?" asked the woman. "The river is too wide. The current is too swift."

The two monks looked at one another in uncertainty, because they had taken a sacred vow to not so much as even touch a woman. Then, without a word, the older monk picked up the woman and carried her across the river, setting her down on the other side. He returned to where his companion was waiting and they carried on.

The younger monk was flabbergasted. He couldn't believe what had happened. He was speechless, and an hour passed without a word between the two of them. Two hours passed. Three hours. Four hours, and finally the younger monk could contain himself no longer. He turned to his fellow monk and blurted out, "How could you have done that? How could you have carried that woman?"

"Oh?" replied the older monk, "Are you still carrying her? I put her down four hours ago."

Zen parable

How much are we carrying around inside us that should have been put down a long time ago? How many past mistakes, regrets, missed opportunities; how much guilt and anger? And how long are we going to carry these toxic attitudes? Are we going to carry them inside us our whole life?

We need to let go, to become freer and lighter. Give it all away. If our mind is filled with regrets, resentments, fear, anger, there is no room for happiness. We're already full. We have to clean house internally. We have to make room within ourselves for inner peace and happiness. You cannot be happy and sad at the same time. You cannot have anger and inner peace simultaneously. You cannot be both positive and negative about the future. Something has to be given away.

> *If your everyday life seems poor, don't blame it;*
> *blame yourself; admit to yourself that you are not*
> *enough of a poet to call forth its riches, because*
> *for the creator there is no poverty*
> *or no poor indifferent place.*
>
> RAINER MARIA RILKE

Inner harmony comes from recognizing that certain attitudes put us in harmony with life and others do not. It comes from noticing how we feel when we think in certain ways. Anger, guilt, fear, worry, self-doubt, disrespect for ourselves or others–these attitudes almost always cause us problems. We should be aware when we slip into these states of consciousness.

Practice monitoring your moods and observing how your mind shifts moment by moment. Happy, sad, overwhelmed, depressed, worried, excited, grateful, bored, amazed–the mind fluctuates between them all.

*If you love peace, then hate
injustice, tyranny and greed–but
hate these things inside yourself,
not in another.*

GANDHI

Notice how each makes you feel. Practice cultivating those feelings that make you feel good, and giving away those that don't.

If you find that you worry a lot, why not give it away? It can be done. I know a man who one day decided to give up worry. He looked at it rationally and realized it never did him any good. He decided that if he were concerned about something, he would come up with a solution, act, or simply let it be. But worry, he realized, was always negative, self-defeating and counterproductive. So he gave it up. Just like that.

If you find yourself always critical of people, give it away. Give away your self-criticism too, and your regrets. Give away goals that no longer have any meaning for you. Give away everything that is holding your destiny and happiness hostage.

The world is now too dangerous for
anything less than utopia.

BUCKMINSTER FULLER

creative
choices

creative
actions

I'm petrified.

I don't think I've ever been more nervous in my life. It is ten minutes to eight, and in ten minutes I'm scheduled to give my first public talk. I've been researching the mind and its powers for three years, and this is my opportunity to finally share what I've discovered. But now I'm wondering what I've gotten myself into.

I peek into the room and see that it is filling up. Returning backstage, I anxiously review yet again the speech I have been practicing for weeks. I have memorized my presentation word for word. It is the classic beginner's mistake, but I won't discover this until it's too late.

I am introduced to polite applause and, looking out at the audience, I see everyone staring up at me. This unnerves me a little but, recovering, I begin my memorized speech. Two or three sentences into my talk, my mind goes completely blank. I freeze and look at the audience in horror.

They look back at me. I feel like a deer caught in the headlights of an onrushing car. Can they see my fear? I don't have a clue what to say next. I'm living my worst nightmare. Fortunately there is a blackboard behind me. I turn to write something, anything to give myself a reprieve from the audience's unrelenting stare. I write slowly, trying desperately to remember what to say. I'm not even sure what I'm writing–some nonsense. How long can I keep writing? I dread turning to face the audience. I just want to go home and hide. But I have no choice.

I turn. People are frowning. I mumble something. Someone gets up and leaves. I'm paralyzed, my mind still a blank. I don't know what to do. "Any questions?" I ask, feebly. My presentation has lasted less than a minute. People leave in disgust. I return that evening to my cabin completely humiliated.

I have previously booked two speaking dates, assuming I was going to give a successful presentation. Now, to my dismay, there is still one more to do. I have the option to cancel it, or to try to somehow make it work. I don't want to face another audience, but I know that if I give up I'll probably never speak in public again. My anxiety is overwhelming, and then I remember the old saying, "Get right back on the horse that has thrown you." Fighting my fear, I resolve to try again.

I have three days to prepare for my second talk. Hopefully, no one there will know of my earlier debacle. I scrap the word-for-word approach and write different topic headings on cue cards to help me. This time I give a very mediocre presentation, stammering and pausing a number of times, but, mercifully, I get through it, and no one leaves. Instead of being disappointed with a mediocre presentation, however, I'm ecstatic. Driving back to the cabin that night I'm thinking, "I've gone from terrible to mediocre! I'm on my way." I sing the entire way home.

> *To change one's life start immediately*
> *No exceptions (no excuses).*
>
> WILLIAM JAMES

Our choices and actions are ultimately what create our life. The law of cause and effect is at work in our lives just as it is everywhere else in the universe. Creative action directed towards any goal will always produce a result. Perhaps the result is not what we originally expected. Quite often, as our paths unfold, new twists present themselves in ways we could never have imagined. But action is always the vehicle that will take us where we want to go.

Looking back over twenty years to that first public talk, I am amazed at how my life has developed. I now regularly speak to audiences of a thousand or more, without any appreciable anxiety. But I am also acutely aware that my first public talk, as humiliating as it was, was the seed of who I am today.

How life unfolds is not so mysterious when we stop to examine our choices and actions. This is why old people have wisdom. They can see clearly how it all developed and why. But young people can discover this too. Look closely at your choices and actions and you will be amazed. Doing so, we discover we have power we did not suspect. Free will and the

{ *The opportunity to become who we want lies in this very moment's behaviour.* }

DAVID REYNOLDS

power to act are not to be taken lightly. The power to mold and create our life is within our grasp. No situation is hopeless or without options. No dream is unattainable. When we are creative with our life we can do anything.

Procrastination is the enemy of change and action. "The time is not right," we say to ourselves. "I'll do it later," we promise. Here I will share with you a secret. The time is never right. There will always be reasons why not to do what you know is important to you. Family, friends, responsibilities, all manner of perceived barriers will always be there blocking you. And when they're gone new ones will appear. Never mind the obstacles–just do it.

Irish Nobel Peace Prize laureate Betty Williams tells the story of how one afternoon while walking home she witnessed a bomb blast where several people died. One little girl's legs were severed and thrown across the street. The girl died in Williams' arms, bleeding profusely.

Williams went home in shock and despair. There was nothing anyone could do, least of all her, but the horror of the incident haunted her. Later that evening, the full impact of what she'd seen shook her into action. Without stopping to consider the consequences, she began knocking on strangers' doors crying out, "What kind of people have we become that we would allow children to be killed on our streets?"

All through the night she tirelessly banged on doors. Gradually the city awoke and rallied around her call. By dawn there were over 15,000 names on petitions, and the peace movement in Northern Ireland was born.

We should welcome the opportunities to act as they present themselves to us daily. They are our chance to create our life. To make changes in our society. To fulfill our destiny. We can do nothing about the past; it has come and gone. We can do nothing about the future, it is not yet here. But today is ours to use in whatever way we choose. Today is the womb through which the future will emerge.

—

A Zen master worked daily in the monastery's garden even though he was well into his nineties. His disciples, seeing how frail he was, begged him to stop, but he would not listen to them. Finally, in desperation, they hid his tools. The master looked for his tools and, unable to find them, he returned to his room. Feeling pleased with themselves, they brought him a hot meal, but he refused it.

Later that evening they came back with another meal and again he refused it. The next day the same. The disciples became worried.

"Why will you not eat?" they asked.
"No work, no eat," was his simple reply.
Reluctantly they gave him back his tools and he returned to the garden. That evening he resumed eating.

Zen parable

We are called to act at all stages of our life, and when we awaken to the power of action, when we act upon our deepest impulses and charge off in the direction of our dreams, we are amazed at how well it all turns out. But first we must act. Practice finding meaningful actions today that move you toward that which is most important to your heart. Trust this power of choice and action that you have been given.

All action contains within it
the seed of gratification.

Creative action not only brings about future accomplishments, but immediate benefits as well. There is satisfaction at all stages of our work when we do it well, putting our heart and soul into the task that is before us.

Brother Lawrence, the seventeenth century Christian mystic, devoted himself fully to the daily task of feeding the brothers at his monastery. He so devoted himself to his job as cook that he eventually perceived no difference between prayer time and work time. His work was his prayer, and he did it with gratitude and love. Each day became an opportunity for him to do his job well, and, instead of seeing this as a chore, his job became a source of immense joy and satisfaction to him. He did it with such love and devotion that it became his path to enlightenment.

So too as salesmen, computer programmers, nursery school teachers or car mechanics; whatever our occupation, we can use our actions as a way of nourishing ourselves as well as helping others. Even the most mundane job has dignity if approached with the right attitude. I once met a man who spent most of his working life at a General Motors assembly plant, putting doors on cars. That was his job. A partially assembled car would come to his area and he and his partner would bolt on the doors. Day after day, month after month, year after year, that's all he did. I wondered how he could even stay at such a job. His answer was a revelation to me.

"Every time I put on a door," he said, "I think to myself, someone is going to get this new car and it is going to bring them pleasure. I am part of bringing them pleasure. Maybe it will be a retired couple. Maybe

HAPPINESS

Bonheur

{FRENCH}

a family, or someone starting a new job. As I put on the door I think of them and bless the car. I wish them safe driving and success and happiness in their lives. By putting on this door I feel in some small way I'm helping and touching them in their lives." I've never forgotten that. All our actions benefit someone in some way and can therefore be a source of nourishment to us.

Each of us is called to enjoy the life we've chosen and to find actions that fulfill our destiny. But destiny is not just what will happen to us in the future. It is also what is happening to us today, and here we must be diligent to ensure we do not miss what is right in front of us. We can, with practice, learn to shift our perspective so that we flow with what each day brings us. We can learn to allow each day, each action to be whole and complete in itself.

Sue Bender, author of *Plain and Simple,* describes a conversation she had with a sculptor friend of hers. He explained his attitude toward creating his art:

"It is the enjoyment of every step in the process of doing–everything, not only the final piece we label art. If accomplishing is the only goal, all that it takes to reach that goal is too slow, too fatiguing–an obstacle to what you want to achieve.

"If you want to rush to the accomplishment, it is an inevitable disappointment. Then you rush to something else. But if every step is pleasant, then the accomplishment becomes even more so, because it is nourished by what is going on."

Practice enjoying each step of your unique life unfolding. A gardener who loves his garden enjoys every stage of the process. The planting of the bulbs, the first shoots, the daily caring for the garden, and the eventual flowering and harvest. So too we can learn to enjoy the process of growing and nurturing our life's adventure.

Regularly acknowledging ourselves for jobs well done can help us appreciate our daily situations. In hunting tribes, when the hunting party brought back a slain animal there was great festivity and celebration to honor the event and the hunters. The tribe would eat because of the hunters' cunning and strength, and this was fully acknowledged. Do we acknowledge ourselves in this way? Perhaps we should.

We are here to do,
And through doing to learn;
and through learning to know;
and through knowing to experience wonder;
and through wonder to attain wisdom;
and through wisdom to find simplicity;
and through simplicity to give attention;
and through attention
to see what needs to be done.

BEN HEI HEI

We can begin by acknowledging the great achievement of earning a paycheck, the modern equivalent of the hunt. There is great honor in feeding your family and maintaining a roof over their heads. We tend to forget this.

> *Good work that leaves the world softer, and fuller and better than ever before is the stuff of which human satisfaction and spiritual value are made.*
>
> JOAN CHITTISTER

Imagine what a difference it would make in our lives if we were honored every payday as a brave and courageous warrior. A feast and celebration in our honor. What strength and power it would give us. Or as parents, once a week a feast with songs praising our patience, our resourcefulness, our ability to get things done despite the numerous distractions. A tribute to us for what usually goes unnoticed and underappreciated.

We all thrive on recognition. And if it's not possible externally at least we can do so internally. We need to honor and respect ourselves for the work we do, to sing our own praises. We are all warriors in our own life adventure, and our daily actions always have meaning and purpose.

Choose wisely and act as if what you do makes a difference. Never let fear or indifference stand in your way. When we awaken to the myriad of possibilities that life affords us and act upon our deepest instincts, we will not be disappointed.

Creative action has power beyond what we understand, and it will always work for our benefit when we choose and direct it wisely. Look at those people who are living meaningful lives and you will see individuals who have found a direction, a purpose, a goal, and are pursuing it. Action is an important part of their lives, and they find satisfaction in the path they have chosen, no matter how humble or mundane it may be.

A happy and meaningful life requires our continuous input and creativity. It doesn't happen by chance. It happens because of our choices and actions. And each day we are given new opportunities to choose and act and, in doing so, create our own unique journey.

But if you have nothing at all to
create, then perhaps you create yourself.

CARL JUNG

loving
kindness...

{ *Love and compassion are
necessities, not luxuries. Without
them, humanity cannot survive.*

THE DALAI LAMA }

I've been visiting

my grandfather at the senior citizens home for some time now. He moved in here when he broke his hip and couldn't look after himself at home anymore.

I go about once a week, and at first I did it as the dutiful grandson, thinking of it as an obligation, but gradually, over the years, I've come to enjoy these visits. We've talked about politics, sports, the weather, his life, my life. I've asked him questions about everything–marriage, sex, health, religion, what's important in life and what's not. I figure that from his perspective he's probably seen and understood more things than a young person like myself could possibly fathom. I want to plumb the depths of the distilled wisdom that's contained within a man who has lived past a hundred.

But now, at one hundred and seven, he hardly talks at all. I'm lucky to get a sentence or two out of him. But still I come. I push him around in his wheelchair, maybe take him out for some fresh air or feed him lunch, and sometimes, when I know he's alert, I'll talk to him about what's happening in my life.

Today, as I sit beside him, his eyes are glazed and he's showing no sign of even recognizing that I'm here.

"Grampa, can you hear me?" I ask for the third or fourth time. No reply. I've brought my newly published book and want to read him a section where he is mentioned. He doesn't know about the passage and I wanted to surprise him with it. But now I'm feeling I've left it too late.

I decide I'll read it anyway. What have I got to lose? "Why don't people use praise more often?" I begin, quoting one of my grandfather's favorite expressions. The passage goes on to say how people respond more favorably to praise than criticism, and it's written from my grandfather's perspective. I continue to read, unsure if he's hearing or not, but then I look up to see him smiling, with tears in his eyes. He's not saying anything, but I suddenly know he's hearing every word.

Somehow sensing that this might be the last time I see him alive, I pour out my feelings. How much he's meant to me. What I've learned from him. How much I love him. I take his limp hand into mine and just sit with him in silence.

"Grampa I've got to go," I finally say, but I don't go. I just sit there looking at his one-hundred-and-seven-year-old face.

Finally I do leave, and as I'm driving away, I'm thinking about how much these weekly visits have meant to me. I know he heard me today and that the reading truly touched him. I know it made him feel good, and this makes me feel fantastic. My visit brought some joy into his life, but it's brought immense joy into mine.

As I stop at a traffic light I also realize that, all these years when I thought I was helping him, he was helping me. I was the real beneficiary of these visits. Whatever he received, I received tenfold, and it's only now that I'm realizing it.

He died a few days later.

Goodness is its own reward.

When we help others we are actually helping ourselves. The joy and happiness that love and compassion for others bring is one of the best-kept secrets of humanity. The benefits are so enormous and consistent that you have to wonder why we don't practice such kindness more often. Helping others always makes us feel good.

Think back to times when you've given of yourself completely. Maybe you nursed a sick friend back to health, helped in a soup kitchen, coached the school football team, volunteered to raise money for some charity. How did it make you feel? And why did it make you feel so good? What is there in loving and helping one another that is so nurturing to our souls? Perhaps in doing so we are rediscovering our connectedness to one another. A hidden part of us thrills with joy when we reach out to one another in simple everyday ways.

Ram Dass said it well in explaining what happens when we help one another: "Caring for one another we sometimes glimpse an essential quality of our being. We may be sitting alone, lost in self-doubt or self-pity, when the phone rings with a call from a friend who's really depressed. Instinctively we come out of ourselves, just to be there with her and say a few reassuring words. When we're done, and a little comfort's been shared, we put down the phone and feel a little more at home with ourselves. We're reminded of who we really are and what we have to offer one another."

Unfortunately, our lives are busy. Sometimes we feel there's no time to help. There are always so many things we have to do, and they all seem so important. But if we do not value helping one another; if we do not see this as an important part of our growth and development, what does that say about us? What path are we on if loving kindness is not a part of our journey? Do we really think that making more money, watching another night of TV, or going out to a fine restaurant will ultimately make us happier?

We search for happiness in romance, achievements, possessions, exciting experiences, and all of these bring us some satisfaction, but always more is needed. The paradox is that if we are totally preoccupied with only our own happiness, we will never truly achieve it.

The Japanese have an expression for neurotic self-preoccupation. It is *seikatsu onchi;* a term loosely translated as "tone-deaf about life." This condition has us totally preoccupied with only ourselves. Every event and circumstance in our life is measured by how it affects us personally. Others are not considered. This self-centeredness is the cause of most of our suffering. Think about it. When you're unhappy, are you thinking about yourself or others? Always yourself. This should teach us something.

HAPPINESS

{ J A P A N E S E }

> { *Goodwill is the mightiest practical force in the universe.*
>
> TALMUDIC PROVERB }

The world mourned the passing of Mother Theresa, and rightly so, but the truth is that there are thousands of unknown Mother Theresas working out there, helping to make our world a kinder and gentler place. Emelda Damani is one of them.

Mother Emelda, as everyone calls her, founded and operates the "Welcome Home Centre," a drop-in shelter in downtown Johannesburg. A devout Christian, she ministers to the homeless and most destitute not with religion, but with love.

Each day, as her doors open at 7 A.M., people drift in for some coffee and a place to relax, but mostly for Mother's love. I was helping there one day and watched while she brushed the hair of a young prostitute, listening to the girl describe her night's exploits and traumas. When the girl finished, Mother embraced her, wrapping her arms around the young

Do all the good you can, by all the means you can,
In all the ways you can, in all the places you can,
At all the times you can, to all the people you can,
As long as ever you can.

JOHN WESLEY

woman, and simply said, "Mother loves you." No advice. No condemnation. Just unconditional love.

"The centre is called the Welcome Home Centre because everyone is welcome," Mother Emelda says. "Many people are hurting. I am just one woman. I cannot help everyone, but everyone who comes here I will love."

The practice of loving kindness is simply being open and responsive to others. It is helping one another through small acts of kindness and compassion. Not once in a while, but regularly and consistently, so we lose our sense of isolation and begin to feel our oneness, and the joy that such oneness brings.

Our mind may try to conceptualize the idea that, "We are all one," but we can never know this with only our mind. Not even an enlightened mind can know this. But our heart knows this truth intimately.

The practice of loving kindness involves loving ourselves as well. Compassion is not just for others, but for ourselves too. In many ways it must start with ourselves. For until we can love and appreciate ourselves, we cannot love and appreciate others. We must learn to see ourselves without the harsh glare of self-criticism, and come to the conclusion that we are good and worthy in who we are now, just as we are now.

This is not always easy. We live in a society and culture that holds up almost impossible ideals that we think we have to match. The millionaire, the celebrity, the beautiful model; success is often measured in what you've achieved, how much money you make or how good-looking you are. And if we fall short of these ideals we deem ourselves unworthy. It is time to awaken from this nightmare. We have spent most of our lives struggling to be something different from what we are, to have more money, be more successful, better looking, smarter, thinner, more fit. In doing this we have too often created a sense of inferiority in who we are now.

I am looking at the flowering dogwood tree through my window this beautiful spring morning. It is blooming magnificently. I have had my coffee and am preparing to write but there it is, demanding my attention, and I am seduced. Each year it seems to flower more and more gloriously, and this morning it is really putting on a show. I'm just sitting here and enjoying it immensely. I am not examining it minutely for every little flaw, though I'm sure there are some. I do not say this flower is beautiful but that one is so-so, and this one could be bigger and that one not so nice. Or this branch is too weak, that one too short, this one too long and looks funny, out of place. I do not. I just sit and appreciate it for what it is, enjoying it immensely.

I can sit and enjoy the beauty of the dogwood, but not the beauty of me. What is wrong here? Am I less than the dogwood tree? What is this neurotic self-examination, this fault-finding, nit-picking feeling going on inside me that makes me feel ashamed, not good enough, unworthy, inferior? Why must I be anything other than what I am?

from A Vision of Power & Glory

A great many of our problems in life occur because we don't always appreciate ourselves. Developing appreciation for ourselves allows us to see our potential as well as our problems. We discover that even though we're not perfect, there is still immense value and beauty in who we are. This is reassuring. Being open and honest with ourselves helps us to be open with others. We learn that we can relate with others on the basis of the goodness and beauty we discover in ourselves. And doing so, the results in our life are both enormous and startling.

When my daughter was small she got the dubious part of the Bethlehem star in a Christmas play. After her first rehearsal she burst through the door with her costume, a five-pointed star lined in shiny gold tinsel designed to drape over her like a sandwich board. 'What exactly will you be doing in the play?' I asked her. 'I just stand there and shine,' she told me. I've never forgotten that response.

Sue Monk Kidd

When we open our hearts large enough to include ourselves and let go of our harsh judgments, something wonderful happens within. We flower and grow strong in this ever-present love and acceptance. Our inner light burns brighter and we are amazed to see ourselves as special and unique, to see our true worth.

The practice of nourishing ourselves and others in this way allows us to become strong and self-assured. Unconditional, total love is called for. No part of ourselves or others is to be omitted. Even the unappealing parts are to be loved and accepted. This is the challenge. And when we rise to the challenge, great alchemy takes place. There is a new dawning. A life without shame or judgment. A life nourished from within. A life of self-acceptance. A life of loving kindness towards all.

Small service is true service.

fun... joy...
& nonsense

{ *There must be quite a few things a hot bath won't cure, but I don't know many of them.* }

SYLVIA PLATH

I am facilitating a

weekend retreat with thirty-five participants, and while the mood is generally upbeat, sometimes things can get serious and heavy. Like right now.

A woman has just finished sharing a very traumatic experience, and our hearts and minds are all with her. It has been talked out and there is nothing more to say. Everyone is silent and reflective.

I've been in this situation often enough to know that right now the very best remedy available is an ample dose of fun and nonsense. I saunter over to a box where various items are kept, pull out a court jester's hat my wife has made for just such occasions, and put it on. The bells on each tri-corner ring softly as everyone in the group looks on in disbelief. I look ridiculous.

We are at a small resort town in New Zealand which overlooks the ocean. There is a lovely grassy field just outside, and I tell them that they are all now to follow me out to that area.

Once outside, I inform them that I am now the "Master of Nonsense," and that we are going to play a game. "It begins with one person who is the amoeba. The amoeba then captures another person; they capture a third and then a fourth. Then... " I say in mock horror, eyes wide for emphasis, "once there are four amoebas, they split into two groups each, who each capture two more, and now there're four groups of amoebas on the loose!"

Boundaries are defined, one person is picked as the amoeba, and the game begins. Immediately the rest of the group moves in unison, like a school of fish, avoiding the oncoming amoeba. I've played this game countless times, and every time I enjoy it as much as I did the first time. Seeing grown adults squeal with excitement is just too much fun to miss.

While it is quite easy to avoid one amoeba, it gets far trickier as they multiply. Some participants who seemed reluctant at first are now scurrying for their lives. One middle-aged woman in blue slacks is laughing hysterically as a group of amoebas gain on her. A man is climbing a tree trying to escape.

I step back and take it all in. Thirty-five men and women playing like children. It is a wonderful sight. The game lasts less than ten minutes and at its conclusion everyone is laughing and clapping with appreciation.

We return to the conference room with everyone feeling fresh and rejuvenated. I've never known fun to fail to work its magic. It seems to be a cure-all for every situation. It is life's secret elixir.

Why aren't you dancing with joy at this very moment?
This is the only relevant spiritual question.

SUFI SEER PIR VILAYET KHAN

When things are too serious in our life, or we feel stressed or sluggish, we need to call upon our own inner "Master of Nonsense." Maybe he or she will take us out for a walk, or have us put aside that important project that's overdue and take in a double feature at the local movie house. There are hundreds of ways to break the tension and take the pressure off. Sometimes we just have to trust the reckless part of ourselves.

Poet Maya Angelou suggests a day off when things get out of kilter:

Every person needs to take one day away. A day in which one consciously separates the past from the future. Jobs, lovers, family, employers, and friends can exist one day without any one of us, and if our egos permit us to confess, they could exist eternally in our absence.

Each person deserves a day away in which no problems are confronted, no solutions searched for. Each of us needs to withdraw from the cares which will not withdraw from us. We need hours of aimless wandering or spates of time sitting on park benches, observing the mysterious world of ants and the canopy of treetops.

Work is not always required... there is such a thing as sacred idleness, the cultivation of which is now fearfully neglected.

GEORGE
MACDONALD

A day away acts as a spring tonic. It can dispel rancour, transform indecision and renew the spirit.

We need to renew our spirit regularly. A busy life necessitates it. We've become too full of activities. Too serious. Too adult. No wonder kids often think we're dull and boring. In many ways that's what we've become. We should get back to our roots and instincts. Bring in more balance. We need to have more fun, and to do so we have to be more creative and spontaneous; to seize the opportunities life presents us whenever and wherever we find them.

injabulo

{ZULU}

It was a somber ceremonial affair honoring the year's Nobel laureates. Many dignitaries were in attendance including Nelson Mandela, Desmond Tutu (winner of the Nobel Peace Prize), the Dalai Lama and various others. The Dalai Lama was standing directly behind Bishop Tutu, who was sitting in a heavy wooden, straight-backed chair. At a particularly earnest moment of the proceedings, Bishop Tutu's hat was abruptly pushed down over his eyes. The Bishop was startled, but didn't have to look back to know who was responsible. The Dalai Lama was laughing. A little practical joke by the Dalai Lama gave a moment of levity to a highly serious affair. The press snapped pictures and the next day, in all the major newspapers, people everywhere saw a picture of Desmond Tutu, his broad smile visible below his crumpled hat, and behind him the Dalai Lama, laughing. The world was able to share in the joke.

That the Dalai Lama did this doesn't surprise me in the least. My few times in his presence have convinced me he's a jokester. I was once at a lunch with the business community of Toronto where the Dalai Lama was being honored. Representatives from various religious groups, business movers and shakers, and numerous local celebrities were in attendance.

The Dalai Lama sat at the head table, holding court, and throughout the meal he had everyone around him laughing. When it came time to speak, however, he spoke very eloquently and with emotion about the plight of the Tibetan people under Chinese rule. What impressed me most about the event was that, even with the obvious burden he felt in his heart for his people and homeland, the Dalai Lama could still so easily find time for joy and laughter.

Nothing is more therapeutic
than a good laugh.

DR. BERNARD JENSEN

The Dalai Lama has a lot to teach us in this regard. The seriousness of life's problems does not have to eliminate our fun and joy. In life it's necessary that we be, at different times, both serious and silly. Typically we've mastered the serious side very well. It's time to explore the wisdom and pleasure of the silly. We often forget that within all spiritual teachings there is a very clear emphasis on the importance of being joyful. Fun, joy and happiness are spiritual principles.

Here children can teach us a lot. In the Bible we read that, "Unless ye become as little children ye cannot enter the kingdom of heaven." What does this mean? What is it about children that we are to imitate? Their trusting nature? Their innocence? The way they live life moment by moment? Certainly all these things, but what about children's most natural instinct, that of having fun? Look closely and you will see fun and joy springing eternally from within them. Children point the way.

Spontaneity, creativity and the ability to let go and have fun are all lessons children can teach us. We would be wise to watch closely how well they master and perform these activities, how they can make fun out of almost anything. In these activities they are the teachers and we are the students.

Take the lesson of spontaneity, for example. I don't think that the Dalai Lama premeditated pushing Desmond Tutu's hat, that he was waiting for just the right moment. It

was undoubtedly a spontaneous impulse, mischievous and fun loving. And to his credit he didn't feel the need to keep it in check; he simply allowed it to happen.

Having fun daily, even if it's only for a few minutes, is a life-affirming practice. It's also a powerful symbol to our subconscious. It is saying I am worthy. Life is good. Even small amounts of fun every day can have a profound effect. We must be diligent in taking the time to nourish ourselves. If, no matter how busy we are, we still have the wisdom to take time for ourselves, we will be well compensated. Don't be fooled by pressures and responsibilities; they will wait for you. We set the agenda for our life, and in our agenda there must always be time for fun.

Practice being spontaneous. Surprise yourself by being "childlike" sometimes. Let each day hold a gift or two for you. Practice bringing fun, joy and nonsense into your life each day. When you find yourself wondering should I, shouldn't I–don't hesitate–do it!

There is an Apache legend that states the Creator created the human beings and gave them the ability to see and talk and hear and think. Then he gave them free will, but still something was missing. He thought for a while and realized what it was. Finally he gave them the ability to laugh and have fun, and only then did he consider that the human beings were complete.

{ *Celebrating a birthday is exalting life and being glad for it. On a birthday we do not say, "Thanks for what you did or said, or accomplished." No, we say "Thank you for being born and being among us."* }

HENRY J.M. NOUWEN

choose
happiness

{ *Our life is an endless journey.*
Our journey consists of constant
ups and downs, hope and fear,
but it is a good journey. }

CHÖGYAM TRUNGPA

My initial instinct

about Eddie has proven correct. There is something very special about him. Anyone who spends time in Eddie's company soon realizes that he is a man who understands life and lives it well.

It isn't just what he says or does; it is more how you feel when you're around him. He always makes you feel comfortable, welcome, at ease in his presence, just as he did when I first sailed with him off Saltspring Island.

But it is more than this too. His whole being seems to radiate peacefulness. And just being in his presence you pick up on that peacefulness, like piano keys resonating with a tuning fork. If you spend time with Eddie, his energy begins resonating within you, and I am not the only one to notice it.

And then there's his attentiveness. Whether he is washing the dishes, talking to his children, fixing a radiator leak in his car, or building a boat, it is done with the utmost attention, as if that action or moment is the single most important thing in his life. He is a true craftsman, always completely present in whatever action he performs. And it all seems so effortless and easy and natural for him. He is the most relaxed and happy person I have ever met.

I bought the *Akimbo* from Eddie shortly after we first met, and since then we've become close friends. We continue to go sailing together, often meeting after his shift at the lumbermill to go for an evening sail, watching the sun go down over the Gulf Islands.

But tonight will be my final night with Eddie for some time. I leave tomorrow for Sydney on a one-year round-the-world lecture tour. We are at his home, cleaning up after the evening meal; I'm rinsing the dishes and he is stacking them in the dishwasher. Elaine, his wife, is in the next room playing with the kids; we can hear their shrieks of laughter. I realize this is the perfect time to ask him a question that's been on my mind for months.

"What's the secret of your happiness?" I ask, feeling a little ridiculous for asking such a question. But I seriously want to know.

"The secret of happiness?" he repeats in mock seriousness. Then, smiling, he says, "There is a secret." Then what seems like the longest pause I've ever experienced transpires. Finally he breaks the silence.

"The secret of happiness can be summed up in one sentence," he says softly, almost conspiratorially. "Once you know the secret you have the key to happiness. Listen carefully, I'm only going to say it once." I instinctively lean forward so as not to miss a word.

"If you want to be happy then... be happy."

I wait for more. There is no more.

"That's it," he says, his voice almost whispering now. "Happiness is a choice." A huge smile again covers his face. He pats me gently on the shoulder and leaves the room.

It is a profound moment in my life because I know he is absolutely right. It really is that simple, and I laugh out loud. Eddie comes back into the room. We make eye contact and he laughs too. We're both laughing now; no more words are needed. His kids burst in wearing their pajamas and begin laughing and shrieking and jumping all over him. Elaine appears at the doorway and the two of us watch and smile as Eddie somehow manages to simultaneously give both of his kids a piggyback ride in the direction of their bedroom.

Later that evening, with the kids asleep, Eddie shares with me how, after much soul-searching, he has come to the realization that his personal spiritual path is simply joy and happiness. "It is my gift to my family. It is my gift to myself and it is my gift to God," he says matter-of-factly. "I practice it the way some people practice prayer or meditation. It is my prayer and meditation."

I've never forgotten that. Eddie's path was to practice happiness.

> *Before enlightenment: chop wood, carry water*
> *After enlightenment: chop wood, carry water.*
> *This is it!*

ZEN PROVERB

Like many great truths, the secret Eddie shared with me is uncomplicated and powerful. He was right. It can be stated in one sentence: Happiness is a choice. It seems too simple, and yet when you examine life closely, it is undeniably true. This is why someone who is homeless can be happy, while someone else who seemingly has everything is miserable.

There will always be numerous reasons in your life to be either happy or unhappy. Each day of your life offers an abundance of rationales to support whatever position you choose. If you want to be happy, look at your life and find reasons to be happy. If you want to be unhappy, then you will likewise find many reasons to be unhappy. It's your choice.

This, then, is the final practice. The practice of choosing happiness. I have left this practice to the end, but in many ways it is the first and most important practice of all, for without mastering this practice, all of the others are useless.

A group of monks meditated each day in the monastery and each wondered when and if they would ever become enlightened. They continued to meditate each day. One morning they heard that one of them had become enlightened and that the Roshi of the monastery had verified it the night before. (In the Zen tradition you must have your enlightenment verified, as it is easy to deceive yourself.)

The monks rushed to seek out the newly enlightened monk. Finding him in the garden, they asked excitedly, "Is it true? Have you become enlightened?"

"Yes, it is true" he answered humbly.

HAPPINESS

zufriedenheit

{GERMAN}

"How wonderful!" they exclaimed in unison. "Tell us, how do you feel?"
"Oh... miserable as ever," he responded.

Zen parable

I love that parable. It shakes the senses and pulls the foundation out from beneath us, exactly as it is meant to. We expect the lucky monk to answer that enlightenment is beautiful, serene, blissful. We are not prepared for his answer. It makes us re-examine our whole concept of enlightenment. Maybe we've been expecting and looking for the wrong things? Another Zen saying states the same thing in a slightly different way: "After enlightenment: laundry." In other words, day-to-day life goes on. Don't expect life to be suddenly perfect, at any time. So too with happiness. Maybe we've been looking in the wrong places.

Zen masters spend many years meditating in order to become enlightened, and then they become enlightened and their enlightenment is often expressed as, "This is it!" They get it. Life is what is right in front of us now. Life is happy. Life is sad. Life is sickness. Life is health. Life is failure. Life is success. It is all life. You cannot take it apart. Each of our lives contains an incredible range of experiences. Some will be tremendously

{
Don't it always seem to go
that you don't know what
you've got till it's gone.

JONI MITCHELL
}

enjoyable and others will be terrible. That's life. It's a package deal.

Remember when you were growing up and you imagined what it was going to be like when you were an adult? Well, guess what? You're all grown up and this is it! But it's different than what you thought it would be. Yes, life never matches what we think it could be, should be, will be. These projections keep us from seeing what is truly going on here and now. Let go of all that and look in front of you. This is it!

One of the biggest reasons we become unhappy and stuck in our life is that we fall into the trap of playing the "I will be happy when" game. By playing this game we delude ourselves into believing that it is our circumstances that are keeping us from being happy, and that when these particular circumstances change, we will finally be happy.

It's a no-win game and it goes like this:

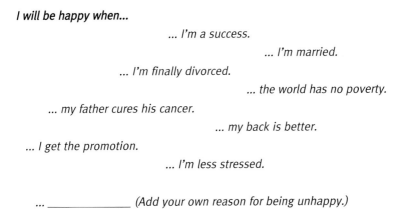

I will be happy when...

    ... I'm a success.

      ... I'm married.

  ... I'm finally divorced.

       ... the world has no poverty.

 ... my father cures his cancer.

     ... my back is better.

... I get the promotion.

   ... I'm less stressed.

... _____ (Add your own reason for being unhappy.)

As soon as life is different, changes, matches our expectations, we reason, then we will be happy. But no matter what we achieve, something else always comes along to provide us with new reasons to be unhappy. Trying to make life fit our expectations is like trying to count to a million. It's going to take a long, long time and will probably never happen. Why not be happy now?

At one point or another we have to accept personal responsibility for uplifting our own lives. No one else can do it for us. We have a life and are living it now. It is wondrous, exciting, frightening, overwhelming, confusing, mysterious, and it is happening to us moment by moment. Our life is a never-ending event, and while we might not always understand it, we can always appreciate it.

All things change and become something else. Nothing stays the same. Life moves forward, and if we do not appreciate what we have now, we might not get another chance to appreciate it. We assume we'll live a long healthy life, that there's lots of time to do what is important to us, and maybe we are right. Then again, maybe you will die tomorrow in a car accident. It's entirely possible. Thousands of people do each year, and none of them planned it.

Several years ago there was a very moving story in the newspaper about a Japanese businessman who wrote a letter to his family during the final twenty minutes of a fatal commercial airliner flight. They were over mountains and he knew a crash was imminent. He also knew his chances of surviving were slight, so he poured his heart out to his wife

and children, all his regrets, all that he hadn't done or said to them. The plane crashed and there were no survivors. The letter was found in the wreckage.

We never know
what tomorrow
will bring,
but we do
have today.

All great artists study and master the techniques of those who have preceded them. Then they can go on to develop their own particular style. So too in life. We can learn from those who have walked this path before. We would be foolish to ignore age-old truths. The path to happiness is well marked for those who wish to embark upon it.

Happiness takes practice, as does anything else you want to be proficient at. A carpenter sharpens his saw and keeps his tools in good condition so that he may be an effective carpenter. He hones his skills by repeatedly practicing them. The more he practices the better he becomes, and a carpenter with twenty years experience is much more accomplished than a novice. The professional dancer who leaps across the stage making it look easy and effortless actually trains extensively–daily exercises, stretches, routines. What looks effortless in fact takes lots of practice.

All spiritual training takes practice too. The Zen master doesn't become enlightened through desire alone. He practices meditation daily until enlightenment happens. The Christian mystic, the Hindu holy man, the North American Indian shaman, all have their practices and disciplines that allow them to progress along their chosen paths. So too with happiness. Practice trusting life and following your call and you will soon find yourself with a fun and interesting life. Practice gratitude and you will be filled with joyful moments. Practice giving away your criticism of yourself and others and you will feel as free and light as a bird in flight. Practice loving kindness and your heart will open and you will come to know your intimate connection to all things. And finally, practice choosing happiness and you will find yourself happy far more often than not.

...and the

The greatest masterpiece of all...
is a life well lived.

journey
continues...

Life unfolds in the most mysterious ways.

My three years in the woods of British Columbia birthed a series of Mind Power seminars which I began teaching in 1978. I first traveled across Canada in 1980, lecturing in all the major urban centers, and in 1981, on February 14 (Valentine's Day), I began my first world tour in Sydney, Australia. Since then I have written four books, and taught hundreds of thousands of people this Mind Power system.

In 1994 I married my wife Sylvia, and we now live in Vancouver, Canada. We have no children but we're still hoping. I continue to write, lecture and teach worldwide, and will probably do so until the day I die.
I love my work.

There is an old proverb that I have always kept close to my heart:
"Blessed is the man who has found his work and one woman to love."

I am a very blessed man.

John Kehoe

Angelou, Maya. *Wouldn't Take Nothing for My Journey Now.* Random House Inc. and Little Brown and Company (UK) London, 1993.

Ban Breathnach, Sarah. *Simple Abundance: A Daybook of Comfort and Joy.* Warner Books, 1995.

Ban Breathnach, Sarah. *Something More: Excavating Your Authentic Self.* Warner Books, 1998.

Barks, Coleman. *The Essential Rumi.* San Francisco, CA: Harper, 1995.

Bartlett, John. *Bartlett's Familiar Quotations.* Little, Brown, 1980.

Beattie, Melody. *Affirming the Good Things in Life.* Harper & Row, 1990.

Bender, Sue. *Plain and Simple: A Woman's Journey to the Amish.* Harper Collins Publishers Inc., 1989.

Caddy, Eileen. *Opening Doors Within.* Findhorn Press, 1987.

Castendada, Carlos. *The Teachings of Don Juan.* Berkeley: University of California Press, 1968.

Chittister, Joan. *There is a Season.* Orbis Books, 1995.

Christie, Agatha. *An Autobiography.* Berkeley Press, 1996.

Dillard, Annie. *Pilgrim at Tinker Creek.* Harper Collins Publishers Inc., 1974.

Eliot, T. S. *Collected Poems 1909-1962.* Harcourt, 1963.

Field, Joanna. *A Life of One's Own.* J.P. Tharcher, 1981.

Fox, Emmet. *Power Through Constructive Thinking.* Harper Collins, 1989.

Jones, Alison., ed. *Dictionary of Quotations.* Chambers, 1996.

Kehoe, John. *A Vision of Power and Glory.* Zoetic Inc. 1994.

Kidd, Sue Monk. *When the Heart Waits.* Harper Collins Publishers Inc., 1990.

Nouwen, Henri J. M. *Here and Now: Living in the Spirit.* The Crossroad Publishing Company, 1994.

Rilke, Maria Rainer. *Letters to a Young Poet.* Random House, 1934.

Ram Dass and Gorman, Paul. *How Can I Help?* Alfred A. Knopf Inc., 1985.

Reynolds, David K. William. *Pools of Lodging for the Moon.* William Morrow & Company Inc., 1989.

Zoetic Inc. would like to thank the individuals and organizations that kindly contributed to this book. Special thanks to Associated Press, Canadian Press, Reuters and others for the photographs.

Visit with John at Home

As a writer committed to staying in touch with his readers, John Kehoe personally invites you to join him via the Internet to share your questions and observations. Each month, from his home, John will respond to a selection of correspondence on matters of interest to his ever-expanding community of readers and students. You'll also find this exciting new site loaded with important news and information updates, tour schedules, interesting links, and tips on how to get the most out of life!

Contact John by directing your browser to:

www.learnmindpower.com

———

Other books by John Kehoe

Mind Power Into the 21st Century
A Vision of Power and Glory
Money Success & You